50 THINGS
THAT WILL GUARANTEE
"SUCCESS IN LIFE, BUSINESS AND MINISTRY"

BONNIE ETTA, PHD

50 things That will guarantee "Success in life, business and ministry"

This book is written to provide information and motivation to readers. Its purpose is not to render any type of psychological, legal, or professional advice of any kind. The content is the sole opinion and expression of the author, and not necessarily that of the publisher.

Copyright © 2023 by Bonnie Etta, PhD.

All rights reserved. No part of this book may be reproduced, transmitted, or distributed in any form by any means, including, but not limited to, recording, photocopying, or taking screenshots of parts of the book, without prior written permission from the author or the publisher. Brief quotations for noncommercial purposes, such as book reviews, permitted by Fair Use of the U.S. Copyright Law, are allowed without written permissions, as long as such quotations do not cause damage to the book's commercial value. For permissions, write to the publisher, whose address is stated below.

Printed in the United States of America.

ISBN   978-1-64552-171-6   (Paperback)
ISBN   978-1-64552-172-3   (Digital)

Lettra Press books may be ordered through booksellers or by contacting:

Lettra Press LLC
30 N Gould St. Suite 4753
Sheridan, WY 82801
1 307-200-3414 | info@lettrapress.com
www.lettrapress.com

PREFACE

50 things
That will guarantee
**"Success in life, business
and ministry"**

This is the result of my forty plus years in the Lord and ministry. I had to prayerfully put together my personal success secrets and this is inspirational, prophetic and full of life and wisdom. It will certainly take you to a new level in life.

Your long term desires can become a reality; you just need to know how.

"Read this and hear the Lord speaking to you through the pages of this book". Every distorted future can be recreated, restored and regained. See it, believe it, take steps toward it and trust God for it. This is a book to read over and over again.

Dr Bonnie Etta

50 THINGS

That will guarantee
**Success in life, business
and ministry**
Tested and proven

1. **Be Realistic** {Be real} Don't live in a dream world.
The place where spirituality does not work is business. Never do business by faith. Do that which is necessary and trust God. Be a man of faith, be Spirit filled and be realistic.

Seest thou a man diligent in his business? he shall stand before kings; he shall not stand before mean men. Proverbs 22:29.

2. Learn quickly: Quick learning. Slow learners will lose several opportunities in life and they will always be running late. Ask God for the grace to grasp it as fast as possible. Quick learners are always ahead of others.

> *Isaiah 11:3. And shall make him of quick understanding in the fear of the LORD: and he shall not judge after the sight of his eyes, neither reprove after the hearing of his ears:*

3. Keen observation

Learn with your eyes be observant, take pictures with your eyes and be totally aware of your terrain. Observe people, places, things and opportunities.

> *Let thine eyes look right on, and let thine eyelids look straight before thee. Proverbs 4:25*

4. Pray about everything at any time.

Keep constant communication with God about every and any engagement. Talk to God in your heart before any engagement. That silent prayer is powerful.

> *And he spake a parable unto them to this end, that* **men**

ought always *to pray, and not to faint. Lu 18:1*

5. Listen more, talk less

Wise people listen more and talk less. Let every word you speak be purposeful and productive.

> *Seest thou a man that is hasty in his words? There is more hope of a fool than of him. Pr 29:20*

> *Be not rash with thy mouth, and let not thine heart be hasty to utter any thing before God: for God is in heaven, and thou upon earth: therefore let thy words be few. Ec 5:2*

6. Spend quality time alone

Jesus spent a lot of time alone early in the morning. You need time alone for rest and meditation.

> *And when he had sent the multitudes away, he went up into a mountain apart to pray: and when the evening was come, he was there alone. Mt 14:23*

Practice spending quality time alone, no noise, no talking, just silent. The result will be awesome inspirational ideas.

7. Think more, worry less

Thinking is productive reasoning. Pondering, asking yourself questions and seeking answers.

For as he thinketh in his heart, so is he: Eat and drink, saith he to thee; but his heart is not with thee. Pro 23:7

8. Ask serious questions: seek answers

The more questions you ask the more answers you get. The way to know more is by asking questions. Ask life changing questions.

The most famous question in the New Testament: When Jesus came into the coasts of Caesarea Philippi, he asked his disciples, saying, "Whom do men say that I the Son of man am?" Mat 16:13.

What must I do to prosper as a child of God?

What must I do to have money legitimately for the glory of God?

Your life will resemble the questions you asked and sought for answers.
I asked this question several years ago, "What must I do to be free from poverty? Write down your questions, Do text some of your questions?

9. Spend time alone in worship

You attract the nature of what you worship, wow! Is that not interesting? True worshippers have benefits also. Peace of mind, confidence, loyalty, and God's presence. As you submit to God in true worship, you grow in wisdom for life, business and ministry.

Always spend quality time with God before making any major decision

> *And it came to pass in those days, that he went out into a mountain to pray, and continued all night in prayer to God. [13] And when it was day, he called unto him his disciples: and of them he chose twelve, whom also he named apostles. Luke 6:12-13.*

10. Clean your inner man by letting go offenses

Unclutter your mind. Create room for new insight. One divine idea is all you need to transform your life, business and ministry.

> *Psalm 51:10. Create in me a clean heart, O God; and renew a right spirit within me.*

11. Think possibilities
 Matthew 18:12. How think ye? ...
Don't think difficulties. Don't think impossibilities. Take crises out of your mind. Think testimonies. See a way out. Think solutions.

> *And it shall turn to you for a testimony. Luke 21:13.*

Always know that it must end well regardless of the process.

12. See the future and not the past

History is good, but never allow history determine your future. Learn from what happened; gain the wisdom to create your desired future. The picture on your mind should never be from your past, it should be your vision. See the future and let it create a deep impression in your inner man.

> *Moreover the word of the Lord came unto me, saying, Jeremiah, what seest thou? And I said, I see a rod of an almond tree. [12] Then said the Lord unto me, Thou hast well seen: for I will hasten my word to perform it. Jeremiah 1:11-12.*

13. Fear and honor God

Do business with the principle of the fear of the Lord and honor of God as your underlining value.

Because of these values you will approach every situation discreetly and with integrity.

> *By humility and the fear of the Lord are riches, and honour, and life. Proverbs 22:4.*

14. Respect people

Value each person's presence, treat people with love and concern. People matter, make them feel valuable and appreciated. For people to keep on coming again and again, they must have a sense of acceptance and warm welcome. Great customer service is a great factor in customer retainment.

> *For I will have respect unto you, and make you fruitful, and multiply you, and establish my covenant with you. Leviticus 26:9.*

15. Be a human being with feelings

Connect with people, know their pain and learn to relate.

Every problem you solve enriches you in one way or another.

Look at someone's tears filled eyes, and let them know that you truly care.

The people you raised up today, will be the people that will keep you standing tall tomorrow. Let your clients know that you truly care.

> *And Jesus went forth, and saw a great multitude, and was moved with compassion toward them, and he healed their sick. Matthew 14:14*

16. Be a problem solver and promise keeper

Listen to people, work with each person to find the solution.

Be dedicated to to God and available to people.

Don't be too busy with business or ministry and then have no time for people.

And when he had called unto him his twelve disciples, he gave them power against unclean spirits, to cast them out, and to heal all manner of sickness and all manner of disease. Matt 10:1

17. Conceive future problems and seek solutions

God saw the flood coming and he worked with Noah to provide a solution. Revelation of what is ahead of you matters a lot and makes the difference. Foreknowledge in business, life, ministry and in politics gives one extra advantage in the field.

Where there is no vision, the people perish: but he that

> *keepeth the law, happy is he.*
> *Proverbs 29:18*

18. Observe successful people

Find out what makes successful people successful. Discover the culture of success. It is easier to manage poverty that wealth. Find out how to maintain success in life and business. Sustainability is the key to generational wealth.

> *Go to the ant, thou sluggard; consider her ways, and be wise:*
> *Proverbs 6:6*

19. Visit the poor and the under privileged and listen to their stories.

Misfortune, mismanagement, adversities and lack of opportunity are what makes the poor, poor in most countries. Listen to them and be grateful to God. Avoid the pitfalls in life.

> *I returned, and saw under the sun, that the race is not to the swift, nor the battle to the strong, neither yet bread to the wise, nor yet riches to men of understanding, nor yet favour to men of skill; but time and chance happeneth to them all. Ecclesiastes 9:11*

20. Keep updating

There are over 272 Bible verses that deals with the word "new".

Never keep doing the same thing and expect different outcome. Find out what you need to become more competitive, and to be ahead of others in the same field. Updating and upgrading is essential for maximum momentum.

> *But we all, with open face beholding as in a glass the glory of the Lord, are changed into the same image from glory to glory, even as by the Spirit of the Lord.*
> *2 Corinthians 3:18 KJV*

21. Find your path.
Knowing your distinctive calling and assignment is key to doing what you were wired to do. Don't be bound by a cast system; you are different

and your path to achieving success may be totally different from that of your peers and progenitors. Finding out who you are and what you are comfortable doing best is vital in life, ministry and business. "Don't wear your grandfather's shoes, they may not be your size.

> *Now there are diversities of gifts, but the same Spirit. [5] And there are differences of administrations, but the same Lord. [6] And there are diversities of operations, but it is the same God which worketh all in all. 1Corinthians 12:4-6*

22. Know your what/why/how and where

The right product, the right target group, the right strategy, the right market place.

Purposefully position yourself for the results you want.

> *I know that you can do all things, and that no purpose of yours can be thwarted. Job 42:2*

23. Create your life's statement of purpose

Who are you, what do you want out of life? What do you have to market? What is your why?

> *And the Lord answered me, and said, Write the vision, and*

> *make it plain upon tables, that he may run that readeth it. Habakkuk 2:2*

24. Study how money works

You can never succeed broke. You need to learn how to get more money, how to grow your money, how to secure your wealth and create generational wealth. *Give your money assignment.*

> *If then you have not been faithful in the unrighteous wealth, who will entrust to you the true riches? Luke 16:11*

25. Overcome money

Learn how to gain control over money and how to use money for God's kingdom.

Don't be influenced by money, manage it, properly distribute it and use it for the purpose intended. Don't be changed by money, use money to bring change.

> *Be not overcome of evil, but overcome evil with good. Romans 12:21*

26. Overcome arrogance

Arrogance and business doesn't work well. Stay simple and focus on your goals.

Arrogance repels people, arrogance attracts fights, arrogance influences your conversation and affects customer relationship. Overcome it.

By humility and the fear of the Lord are riches, and honour, and life. Proverbs 22:4

Pride goeth before destruction, and an haughty spirit before a fall. Proverbs 16:18.

27. Engage in a cause or mission that transforms people for good.

Define your motivational factor. Commit in something that solves a human problem and gives people opportunity for better life. Seek to be part of something greater than yourself. What can you do for God in your city and for your generation? Find your fulfillment in doing something that benefits others.

Then said I, Lo, I come (in the volume of the book it is written of me,) to do thy will, O God. Hebrews 10:7

28. Study/research in your area of assignment

Study, study, study and keep studying. It will take continuous improvement to be on top in the competitive marketplace. Everything is rapidly evolving. Keep on updating, upgrading and renovating. "If you can not properly package yourself, you would not properly package your products" *Bishop Bonnie Etta, quotes*

Study to shew thyself approved unto God, a workman that needeth not to be ashamed, rightly dividing the word of truth. 2 Timothy 2:15

29. Accept to suffer today and enjoy tomorrow

Every true successful person, works very hard everyday. You can't lazy around and become successful. Even if you inherit a fortune, it will take hard work to sustain it. You would have to fold your sleeves and work like never before. Success is not cheap. No sweat, no success.

> *For I reckon that the sufferings of this present time are not worthy to be compared with the glory which shall be revealed in us. Romans 8:18*

30. Develop the winning mentality

You must win in your mind in order to win in the market place. Failure is not an option, no matter the process be determined to win at the end. Winning mentality is what gives us the courage to hold on until we see the breakthrough.

Winning mentality ends up with victory celebration. Think of Joshua and Caleb in the Bible.

> *And Caleb stilled the people before Moses, and said, Let us go up at once, and possess it; for we are well able to overcome it. Numbers 13:30.*

Keep telling yourself; I am able to...

31. Make the best use of every failure

A failure does not decide your destiny. A failure empowers you to fight the more. Thank God I failed, that is why I succeeded. Make the best use of every challenging moment of your life, and use it as a springboard to rise higher. Every successful person failed before, but refused to end where they failed.

> *And Simon answering said unto him, Master, we have toiled all the night, and have taken nothing: nevertheless at thy word I will let down the net. Luke 5:5*

32. Attend funerals; make everyday count

Don't be deceived by the glamour and fantasy around us. Think on how you want your life to end. To make your life count, think on how fragile life is and make the best decisions by the grace of God. Give your day an assignment.

> *It is better to go to the house of mourning, than to go to the house of feasting: for that is the end of all men; and the living will lay it to his heart. Ecclesiastes 7:2*

33. Make Jesus Christ your Lord and role model

There is no way you can fail in life if you live life as Jesus did. Jesus did not place his priority on the temporal. He focused on what would matter in life and eternity. Jesus Christ is my personal role model. The values of Jesus guarantees excellence in every culture or nation where you find your self. Just love people and that will turn your life and business around. Love never fail…

> *Charity never faileth: but whether there be prophecies, they shall fail; whether there be tongues, they shall cease; whether there be knowledge, it shall vanish away. 1 Corinthians 13:8*

34. Make the Bible your life's manual

Read the Bible to gain wisdom, learn what's right, correct wrong thinking and receive guidance.

> *Thy word is a lamp unto my feet, and a light unto my path. Psalm 119:105*

35. Be fearless, yet humble

know what you want, stand firm and press on. Weak people can't lead. Be an individual with a firm and humble character. Let no challenge break you, don't be shaken in the face of adversity.

> *For God hath not given us the spirit of fear; but of power, and of love, and of a sound mind. 2 Timothy 1:7*

36. Pray and plan

Pray like never before, plan like never before. We pray because we need God's help. We plan because we have a will and we must have a plan to seek God's direction and blessings. Pray-Think-Plan. You are responsible *for your daily schedule, you should bring your vision to God in prayers.*

> *What is your plan for the next Twelve months?*

> *Jesus Christ had a plan: "And it came to pass afterward, that he went throughout every city and village, preaching and shewing the glad tidings of the kingdom of God: and the twelve were with him." Luke 8:1*

37. Praise God in the midst of the storm

Challenges are part of life. We live on mountain top and in the valley. Your find yourself today in the valley? Keep moving, you will soon go through it. You should know that the storm don't last forever. In business or ministry, you will go through several storms in life. Like the palm tree; the storms only make you stronger and causes your roots to grow deeper.

> *Though he slay me, yet will I trust in him: but I will maintain mine own ways before him. Job 13:15*

38. Create your own brand/ don't be a photocopy.

Begin from somewhere and grow; refuse to continue as a consumer, create something. Seek to do something unique: Seek counseling on how to begin your own brand and grow your franchise.

> *According to all that I shew thee, after the pattern of the tabernacle and the pattern of all the instruments thereof, even so shall ye make it. Exodus 25:9*

39. Manage your anger

You can be self control and calm in the face of stressful circumstances. Anger will destroy everything you have labored for. Don't be happy for things that are inappropriate but don't escalate the situation. To build, you will have to learn to tap someone on their shoulder and say, "you can do better than this". Don't let anger destroy the connections you have labored for years to build. Be angry and sin not.

> *Be angry, and do not sin; ponder in your own hearts on your beds, and be silent. Selah. Psalm 4:4*

40. Manage your staff with care and wisdom.

You can never build a growing business alone; you need people, therefore value your staff and relate with each staff with care and wisdom. One of the symptoms of a dying business is that staff come and go, they don't last. Great managers retain hardworking employees and rewards them. Cause people to enjoy working with you and not to endure working with you.

Can two walk together, except they be agreed? Amos 3:3

41. Know that you need people

Besides being a great manager you need to personally know that you need God and you need people. Some people think that all they need is God; that is because they don't appreciate with people do unto them. Someone contributes to *every profit you make. Learn to bold appreciate and encourage your team for greater productivity and excellence.*

> *Greet Priscilla and Aquila my helpers in Christ Jesus: 4. Who have for my life laid down their own necks: unto whom not only I give thanks, but also all the churches of the Gentiles. Romans 16:3-4*

42. Stay focused on your goals

Know what you need to do, do it and move to the next project. Uncompleted projects are wasted resources. Poor neighborhood are identified by the number of abandoned building projects; that means no jobs, no businesses and no progress. Staying focused on your goals propels you for results; achievements means goal attainment. Don't just be busy, get results.

> *I therefore so run, not as uncertainly; so fight I, not as one that beateth the air: [27] But I keep under my body, and bring it into subjection: lest that by any means, when I have preached to others, I myself should be a castaway. 1 Corinthians 9:26-27*

43. Don't be a quitter

Stay on it, master it and win on it. Growth takes time. Real promotion is not for the newly employed, it is for the tested and approved. I tell my associates that, "If you can't suffer with me, you can't enjoy with me". Don't quit on your vision, seek for help and wisdom and make it happen.

> *And let us not be weary in well doing: for in due season we shall reap, if we faint not. Galatians 6:9*

44. Keep studying and keep working hard

Work and study, study and work. You should never graduate from studying and you should never graduate from working. Even after retirement work if you want to be alive. "Death takes over when you stop working".

Whatever your calling and assignment in life is, keep reading, keep working on it and keep growing. Working in ignorance will end up in poverty and devastation.

> *Till I come, give attendance to reading, to exhortation, to doctrine. 1 Timothy 4:13*

45. Purposefully save money

No what you want and save the money for it. To many loans will cripple your business. Give your work assignment, to raise "this" amount of money for "this" purpose. Your financial goals and very important in your life, business or ministry. Not saving money means mismanagement, stagnation, poverty and future devastation. The more the money, the more you can accomplish for the kingdom of God.

Who fed thee in the wilderness with manna, which thy fathers knew not, that he might humble thee, and that he might prove thee, to do thee good at thy latter end; [17] And thou say in thine heart, My power and the might of mine hand hath gotten me this wealth. [18] But thou shalt remember the Lord thy God: for it is he that giveth thee power to get wealth, that he may establish his covenant which he sware unto thy fathers, as it is this day. Deuteronomy 8:16-18

46. See your next move.

Never settle, keep dreaming big, there is still much more ahead of you. Get ready for greater growth, revival, breakthroughs and the manifestation of the glory of the Lord. Keep telling yourself "My future is greater than this". See by faith the future of your cooperation and begin to make it happen. Begin to train for it. I live more in the future than in the present; at the same time I cease every opportunity to make it today. "There is no tomorrow if you can't make it today" Empower yourself to fight the good fight and to win in the market place and in the ministry. See the future God has for you and learn to take giant steps in the name of Jesus Christ. Succeed for the glory of God and for the advancement of God's kingdom.

Thou art worthy, O Lord, to receive glory and honour and power: for thou hast created all things, and for thy pleasure they are and were created. Revelation 4:11

47. Practice tithing with a purpose

And all the tithe of the land, whether of the seed of the land, or of the fruit of the tree, is the Lord's : it is holy unto the Lord. Leviticus 27:30

Miracles through Tithing

1. Tithes is the power behind my financial miracle expectation

2. Tithes is the covenant connection between Abraham and Blessings of the high priest Melchizedek

3. Tithes is the covenant power that secures our investments and the power that guarantees our profit making

4. Tithing is the first and only law God gave to Adam and Eve, everything in the garden belongs to you but this one portion belongs to me. What did Adam and Eve do? The still had to bite the one that belonged to God.

5. Tithing and circumcision are the two covenant sacraments passed down through the Abrahamic linage. The generational blessings of Abraham depended upon these two sacraments

6. Tithing was re-enforced by the law to help Israel acknowledge that they do not despend on their wealth but on the Lord. Nothing will ever be sufficient without the Lord: the Lord is our sufficiency

7. Tithing assigns Angels on our inheritance to guarantee our fruitfulness

8. Tithing assigns Angel to protect our investments from the devourers

9. Tithing empowers our assurance for prosperity

10. Tithing opens our heavens

11. Tithing Opens the windows of heaven for us and brings down our expections.

12. Tithing is the weapon of war against poverty and adversity

13. Tithing is the connection between your money and the store room in heaven. God deposits his money in the bank accounts of those who tithe. So the will never lack money to invest in God's kingdom.

14. Tithing was the secret behind the prosperity of Jacob, he built alters to sacrifice tithes of his cattle to God.

15. Tithing to the God of Abraham is what kept Israel as a nation under God.

16. Tithing is the sign of loyalty to God.

17. Tithing is the acknowledgment that God owns all that I have and all he wants is just 10%

18. Tithing rebukes the devil from all that belongs to you.

19. Tithers harvests favor for life

20. Tithing establishes your faith in the Abraham's blessings.

Let your business tithe to God and submit your business to God.

Jesus Christ is our Melchizedek, our high priest today, he received the first tithe and he is still receiving tithes today through his church.

48. Stay simple but serious
No need to be tensed and stressed. Simplify your life and be cautious. No playing about your business; you are out to make profit. Being simple helps

you to be able to relate to everyone. In business and ministry the more people you connect with the more advantage you have. Make use of every God given advantage, go for it with all boldness and faith.

> *Seest thou a man diligent in his business? he shall stand before kings; he shall not stand before mean men. Proverbs 22:29*

49. Be active in the house of God

Honor God with your worship, serve in the house of God. It's a great privilege to be a blessing in the house of God. Get involved in a department and make a difference through your commitment. One can never be too foolish in life, business and ministry if one sincerely submits and serves faithfully in the house of God. God blesses faithfull service.

> *Trust in the Lord with all thine heart; and lean not unto thine own understanding. [6] In all thy ways acknowledge him, and he shall direct thy paths. Proverbs 3:5-6*

50. Glorify God with all of you and sponsor God's kingdom

My greatest secret: giving God all the glory for what he has done for me and standing as a financial partner for World Missions. The greatest fulfillment I have is to know that my financial contribution is helping someone reconcile with God, that many children have financial support and pastors are trained for effective ministry.

Investing in schools, medical centers, Gospel conferences and changing lives one person at a time. Begin within your local church and grow to become a greater blessing to the needs of the body of Christ. Give your money assignment.

> *Thou art worthy, O Lord, to receive glory and honour and power: for thou hast created all things, and for thy plehaasure they are and were created. Revelation 4:11*

For More information: Contact Dr Bonnie Etta

Email: <u>agborbonnie@gmail.com</u>

Facebook: Dr Bonnie Etta

ABOUT THE AUTHOR

Bishop Bonnie Etta is a multi-talented servant of God. Entrepreneur and the senior pastor and founder of the World Mission international Worship Center-Maryland USA and president of the World Mission International Bible college.

He has served in the past forty years in various mission fields in Africa and Europe and his conference, the World Mission International School of Ministry has healed and restored thousands of souls around the world.

Bishop Bonnie Etta is the author of several inspirational books including the best selling: **"STREE FREE LIFE, Lord Use me, etc". Search for books by Dr Bonnie Etta**

www.ingramcontent.com/pod-product-compliance
Lightning Source LLC
Chambersburg PA
CBHW061731070526
44583CB00024B/3100